THE STORY OF THE

TAMPA BAY BUCCANEERS

By Jim Whiting

Kaleidoscope
Minneapolis, MN

The Quest for Discovery Never Ends

This edition first published in 2021 by Kaleidoscope Publishing, Inc.

No part of this publication may be reproduced in whole or in part without written permission of the publisher.

For information regarding permission, write to Kaleidoscope Publishing, Inc.
6012 Blue Circle Drive
Minnetonka, MN 55343

Library of Congress Control Number 2020936060

ISBN
978-1-64519-247-3 (library bound)
978-1-64519-315-9 (ebook)

FIND ME IF YOU CAN!

Bigfoot lurks within one of the images in this book. It's up to you to find him!

TABLE OF
CONTENTS

KICKOFF!

Many years ago, pirates swarmed through Tampa Bay in Florida. They wore handkerchiefs on their heads. They carried swords. (They probably did NOT say "arrrr!") Another word for pirates is "buccaneers." Today's Tampa Bay Buccaneers wear helmets. They carry footballs. The two groups have one thing in common. They are fierce! Excited fans pour into Raymond James Stadium for the Bucs game. Soon it's time for the kickoff. Will the Bucs make their opponent walk the plank?

FUN FACT

Fans can stand on the ship during games. The cannons fire when the Bucs score!

Chapter 1
Buccaneers History

The Bucs came close to the Super Bowl in their fourth season!

Tampa Bay joined the NFL in 1976. The team wasn't very good. They lost all 14 games in their first season. They didn't win their first game until losing 12 more the next year!

That was about to change. The Buccaneers won 10 games in 1979. They topped the NFC (National Football Conference) Central Division. They played the Los Angeles Rams in the NFC Championship Game. The Rams won 9-0. Tampa Bay won the Central Division again in 1981. The Dallas Cowboys crushed them in the playoffs, 38-0. The Bucs had another playoff loss the following year.

That set off a long dry spell. Tampa Bay had 14 straight losing seasons. Three times they won just two games.

In 1997, Tampa Bay got better. The team had a great defense. It featured tackle Warren Sapp, linebacker Derrick Brooks, and safety John Lynch. The Bucs won 10 games. It was their most wins in 18 years. They lost to the Packers in the playoffs.

The defense led the way again two years later. Tampa Bay won 11 games. It was a new team record. Then they lost to the Rams for the NFC Championship again. The score was 11-6.

Bucs action from a 1999 game

Tampa Bay was in the playoffs again the next two seasons. But both times they lost in the first round. Fans were disappointed.

From a tough start, Tampa Bay had turned into a solid team. Bucs fans saw a lot of big stars and big wins. From 1997 to 2007, the team was in the playoffs seven times!

The Bucs battled the Rams in the 1999 NFC title game.

In 2002, the Buccaneers switched to the NFC South Division. It was a good move! Brooks led one of the NFL's best defenses. Mike Alstott and Michael Pittman powered a tough running game. Veteran Brad Johnson was the QB. He threw only six interceptions all season. It was a winning combination. Tampa Bay won their new division. They beat the 49ers and the Eagles in the playoffs. Led by the defense, the Bucs then won their first Super Bowl!

NO MORE BRUCE!

Tampa Bay's first logo showed Bucco Bruce. He was modeled after a movie star. Bruce wore a plumed hat. His teeth clenched a knife. He even winked. Many people thought Bruce wasn't fierce ednough. In 1997, the team changed the logo. It shows a menacing skull on crossed swords. A football lies between the swords. After the team changed the logo, it started winning!

Tampa Bay fans hoped for a Super Bowl repeat in 2003. But the team only won seven games. Many of the losses were very close. Four were by three points. Another one was by just two.

The Bucs won the NFC South two years later with an 11-5 mark. The main reason was **rookie** running back Carnell "Cadillac" Williams. He rushed for 1,178 yards. He was named Rookie of the Year. In the Wild Card game, the defense held Washington to just 120 yards. But the Bucs committed three **turnovers**. They lost 17-10.

Cadillac Williams

Tampa Bay won the South Division again in 2007. They lost in the Wild Card round to the Giants. It was the last time they were in the playoffs. They won 10 games in 2010. But it wasn't quite good enough. They came close again in 2016. Both Tampa Bay and Detroit had 9-7 marks. The Lions won the tiebreaker.

In 2019, Tampa Bay lost six of its first eight games. They came back to win five of their next eight. Their 7-9 record fell short of the playoffs once again.

Mike Evans is Tampa Bay's top receiver.

TIMELINE OF THE TAMPA BAY BUCCANEERS

1976

1976:
Tampa Bay plays its first NFL season but loses all 14 games.

1979

1979:
Tampa Bay has its first winning season and advances to the NFC Championship game. They lose 9-0 to the Rams.

1997

1997:
Buccaneers' 10-6 record is their best season in 15 years. But they lose to Green Bay in the playoffs.

1999

1999:
Tampa Bay wins team-record 11 games.

2002

2002:
Buccaneers move to the NFC South Division and win the Super Bowl!

2005

2005:
Tampa Bay wins 11 games but loses in the first round of the playoffs.

2007

2007:
Buccaneers win the South Division but lose in the first round of the playoffs.

THE DEFENSE NEVER RESTS

Super Bowl MVP Dexter Jackson holds up the Super Bowl trophy!

TAMPA BAY

Before the 2002 season, Tampa Bay wanted Jon Gruden as their new coach. There was a problem. Gruden coached the Oakland Raiders. The Buccaneers gave Oakland several high draft picks. They also paid $8 million. They got their man!

It was worth it. Tampa Bay won 12 games. That is the most in team history. The Bucs easily advanced to the Super Bowl. They played the Raiders. That was Gruden's old team. People called it the "Gruden Bowl."

The Raiders took an early 3-0 lead. Then the Tampa Bay defense took over. Safety Dexter Jackson intercepted two passes. That helped the Bucs to a 20-3 lead. The Bucs were just getting warmed up. They had three pick-six plays in the second half. They held Oakland to 19 rushing yards for the whole game. Tampa Bay cruised to a 48-21 victory! It was their first Super Bowl win.

Chapter 2

Buccaneers All-Time Greats

Tampa Bay prides itself on great defenses. Lee Roy Selmon was the team's very first draft choice in 1976. His brother Dewey joined the team in the same draft. Lee Roy was named to the Pro Bowl six years in a row! Perhaps the team's best lineman was Warren Sapp. He still holds the team record for career sacks. He was a four-time first team All-Pro. Defensive tackle Gerald McCoy had six straight Pro Bowl appearances between 2012 and 2017.

FUN FACT

Lee Roy's brother, Dewey, was his Bucs teammte for five seasons.

Lee Roy Selmon

Derrick Brooks was Tampa Bay's greatest linebacker. He was named first team All-Pro five times. He was also named to 11 Pro Bowls. He played beside Hardy Nickerson for several years. They gave Tampa Bay a great one-two punch at linebacker.

Derrick Brooks

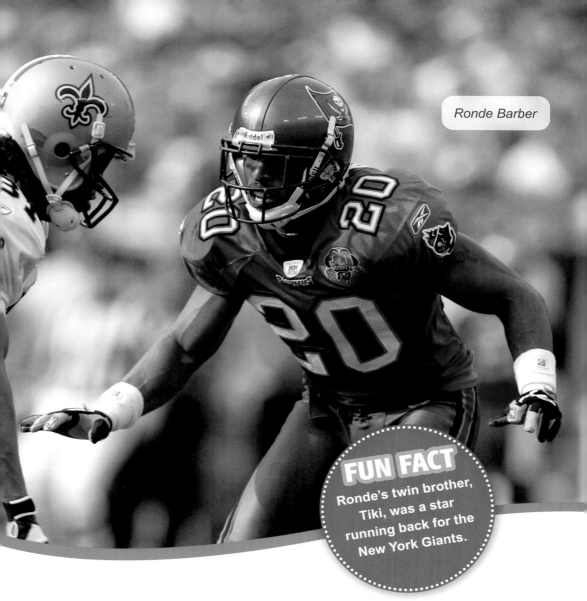

Ronde Barber

FUN FACT

Ronde's twin brother, Tiki, was a star running back for the New York Giants.

Safety John Lynch and cornerback Ronde Barber anchored the secondary. Lynch was one of the hardest-hitting safeties of his era. Barber had 47 career interceptions. He returned eight for touchdowns. He also had four **fumble** returns for touchdowns.

In a game against Minnesota, fullback Mike Alstott caught a pass on the Vikings 10-yard line. He broke one tackle. He ran over a cornerback. He carried a linebacker on his back into the end zone. That was typical of his hard-nosed playing style. He was the last of the great NFL fullbacks. The "A-Train" was a bruising runner. His crunching blocks opened gaping holes for running backs. He hauled in passes. Alstott holds the team record for career touchdowns!

Mike Alstott

BUCCANEERS

RECORDS

These players piled up the best stats in Bucs history. The numbers are career records through the 2019 season.

Total TDs: Mike Alstott, 71

TD Passes: Jameis Winston, 121

Passing Yards: Jameis Winston, 19,737

Rushing Yards: James Wilder, 5,597

Receptions: Mike Evans, 462

Points: Martin Gramatica, 592

Sacks: Warren Sapp, 77

Chapter 3

Buccaneers Superstars

Tampa Bay fans thought their big star in 2020 would be Mike Evans. In six NFL seasons, he has never had less than 1,000 yards receiving. He burst onto the scene in 2014. He had 12 TD catches as a rookie! He has become one of the league's best receivers since. Evans has been named to three Pro Bowls.

Starting in 2020, he had a new QB. The great Tom Brady signed with the Bucs! Brady is known as the GOAT— Greatest of All Time.

With New England from 2000 to 2019, Brady won an NFL-record six Super Bowls. He was the MVP of four of those games. Brady was named to an amazing 14 Pro Bowls!

Mike Evans

Chris Godwin

Winston's great 2019 season had a lot of help. He threw to a pair of great wide receivers. Chris Godwin was in his third season with the Bucs. He became a starter for the first time. He snagged 86 passes for 1,333 yards. Only two other NFL players topped him. Veteran Mike Evans added another 1,157 yards.

Godwin and Evans were joined in 2020 by Rob Gronkowski. The five-time Pro Bowl tight end is back with his old Patriots QB Tom Brady.

Ronald Jones II and Peyton Barber take turns carrying the **rock**. They had almost 1,200 yards between them in 2019.

Peyton Barber

The biggest star on defense is linebacker Shaq Barrett. He had 19.5 sacks in 2019. He became the first Buc to ever lead the league in sacks.

Rookie linebacker Devin White had a great game against Jacksonville on December 1. He intercepted his first pass. Moments later, Barrett **strip-sacked**

Shaquil Barrett

Devin White heads for the end zone.

Jaguars quarterback Nick Foles. White scooped up the loose ball. He raced into the end zone! White did even better in the season's final game. He scooped up another loose ball. He dashed 91 yards for a touchdown. White was clocked at an incredible 21.89 miles per hour!

Tampa Bay fans hope these players can help their team return to the playoffs. Then the next step would be a second Super Bowl victory!

BEYOND
THE BOOK

**After reading the book, it's time to think about what you learned.
Try the following exercises to jumpstart your ideas.**

RESEARCH

FIND OUT MORE. Where would you go to find out more about your favorite NFL teams and players? Check out NFL.com, of course. Each team also has its own website. What other sports information sites can you find? See if you can find other cool facts about your favorite team.

CREATE

GET ARTISTIC. Each NFL team has a logo. The Buccaneers logo shows a pirate flag. Get some art materials and try designing your own Buccaneers logo. Or create a new team and make a logo for it. What colors would you choose? How would you draw the mascot?

DISCOVER

GO DEEP! As this book shows, the Buccaneers had a very tough start. They lost their first 26 games! Think how you would feel if you were on the team. Or if you were a fan, how would keep rooting for them during that long losing streak?

GROW

GET OUT AND PLAY! You don't need to be in the NFL to enjoy football. You just need a football and some friends. Play touch or tag football. Or you can hang cloth flags from your belt; grab the belt and make the "tackle." See who has the best arm to be quarterback. Who is the best receiver? Who can run the fastest? Time to play football!

RESEARCH NINJA

Visit *www.ninjaresearcher.com/2473* to learn how
to take your research skills and book report writing to the next level!

RESEARCH ·

DIGITAL LITERACY TOOLS

SEARCH LIKE A PRO
Learn about how to use search engines to find useful websites.

FACT OR FAKE?
Discover how you can tell a trusted website from an untrustworthy resource.

TEXT DETECTIVE
Explore how to zero in on the information you need most.

SHOW YOUR WORK
Research responsibly— learn how to cite sources.

WRITE ·

GET TO THE POINT
Learn how to express your main ideas.

PLAN OF ATTACK
Learn prewriting exercises and create an outline.

DOWNLOADABLE REPORT FORMS

Further Resources

BOOKS

Cooper, Robert. *Tampa Bay Buccaneers (Inside the NFL).* Minneapolis.: Abdo Publishing, 2019.

Laniness, Katie. *Tampa Bay Buccaneers.* Mankato, Minn.: Big Buddy Books, 2019.

Stewart, Mark. *The Tampa Bay Buccaneers.* Chicago: Norwood House Press, 2019.

WEBSITES

FACTSURFER

Factsurfer.com gives you a safe, fun way to find more information.

1. Go to www.factsurfer.com.

2. Enter "Tampa Bay Buccaneers" into the search box and click 🔍

3. Select your book cover to see a list of related websites.

Glossary

fumble: a ball dropped by a ballcarrrier. White scooped up the fumble and ran to the end zone.

plumed: feathered. The pirate's ostrich feather made his hat a plumed one.

Pro Bowl: the NFL's annual all-star game. Being chosen for the Pro Bowl is a huge honor for any player.

rock: nickname for the football. Barber carried the rock in for six!

rookie: a player in his first pro season. Devin White was Tampa Bay's top rookie in 2019.

strip sack: a tackle of the quarterback behind the line of scrimmage that also results in a fumble. Sapp strip-sacked Brady and the Bucs recovered the ball.

tiebreaker: in the NFL, the stats that determine who makes the playoffs when teams have the same record. Tampa Bay scored more points that season, so it won the tiebreaker.

turnover: losing the ball to the defense by fumble or interception. Every offense wants to avoid turnovers.

veteran: a player with several years of experience. Five-year NFL veteran Mike Evans helps younger players.

Index

PHOTO CREDITS

The images in this book are reproduced through the courtesy of: AP Images: Joe Robbins 4; 6; Kevin Terrell 14; Peter Read Miller 16. Focus on Football: 12, 18, 19, 22, 23, 24, 25, 26. Newcom: Jim Bryant/UPI 8; John W. McDonough/SI 9; Tony Medina/Icon SMI 11; Gary Reyes/KRT 14; Cliff Welch/Icon SW 17, 23; Gary Bogdon/KRT 20; David Rosemblum/Icon SW 27.

About the Author

Jim Whiting lives in Oregon. He has written more than 150 sports books for young readers. He wasn't very good in football when he was growing up. He did better in college. He was captain of his flag football team. One time he scored six touchdowns!